THE OCD COLORING BOOK

Tammy LaBrake, LCSW-R

Illustrations by SDwebcreation

The OCD Coloring Book

Copyright © 2016 by Tammy LaBrake, LCSW-R

Contributors: Illustrated by SD Webcreation. Formatted by Indie Publishing Group

All rights reserved.

The information in this book is not intended as a substitute for consultation with health care professionals. Each individual's health concern should be evaluated by a qualified professional. No part of this book may be reproduced or transmitted in any form or by any means, electronic or mechanical, including photocopying, recording, or by any information storage and retrieval system without the written permission of the author, except where permitted by law.

ISBN 978-0-9983597-0-0

If you are coping with an Obsessive Compulsive Disorder (OCD) then you know how intrusive and demanding OCD can be. The key to beating OCD is knowing how to interact with it. It's important to treat it like a separate entity. It has a distinct and independent existence from you.

The artwork in The OCD Coloring Book will mentally and emotionally immerse you into the much needed practice of "talking back" to OCD. Each image reinforces a strategy that helps you put OCD in its proper place.

The OCD Coloring Book includes a variety of playful, sometimes paradoxical scenes that incorporate therapies such as Exposure & Response Prevention (ERP) and Acceptance and Commitment Therapy (ACT). These therapies are widely recognized as effective treatments for OCD and are explained in The OCD Coloring Book.

This is a beginner's guide for people seeking help with OCD. For those familiar with the treatment of OCD, The OCD Coloring Book can reinforce concepts previously learned and be used as a relapse prevention strategy.

About the Product:

- 14 playful designs based on proven therapeutic strategies.
- Each coloring page is explained by a Licensed Clinical Social Worker who specializes in the treatment of OCD.
- Colored pages and slogans can be displayed and used as visual reminders for daily practice.
- Designed for both beginners and those already familiar with the treatment of OCD.
- Suitable for all ages.

OCD KNOWS NOTHING

OCD has no life experience. That's why it's always asking questions. It can't retain information either, so it can't learn anything. That's why it keeps asking the same questions over and over. Even after you answer its questions, just like a 2 or 3 year old, it keeps asking again and again.

This is the nature of OCD. It has no life experience. No answers. Yet, somehow it manages to boss you around. It does this by tricking you. Every day with OCD is like April Fool's Day. If you know this, you have all the power you need to Boss it Back®.

On April Fool's Day you're fully prepared for the pranks about to be pulled. You're on high alert, vowing to let no one trick you. You say "ha-ha" when somebody tries. No one gets away with it because you're ready for it. This is how you must be every single day with OCD.

If you can agree OCD knows nothing and can't retain information then there's no longer any point in trying to teach it anything. You don't have to prove it wrong or right. You certainly don't have to do what it says. Would you let a 2 or 3 year old boss you around? Of course not! And you wouldn't keep answering the same questions either.

Knowledge is power. Know that OCD is incapable of learning anything. Know that it is a trickster and that every day with OCD is April Fool's Day. Be ready for its pranks and say, "Ha-Ha you can't fool me, OCD."

FEEL THE FEAR AND GO FOR IT

Whatever triggers your fear or discomfort, OCD says, "Stay away! Watch out! Stop! What if…" OCD is a chaperone on steroids.

According to OCD, every trigger is dangerous. Every trigger will lead to a catastrophe. It warns: "You'll be overwhelmed." "It'll be all you can think about." "You'll feel guilty for the rest of your life." "This will cause irreversible damage."

If you're listening to OCD, then you're the one giving it steroids. On steroids it's only going to be more hyper-vigilant. The thoughts will accelerate. The urges will intensify. However, if you feel the fear and go for it, OCD actually decelerates. The thoughts slow down and the urges become less intense.

When you feel the fear and go for it, at first OCD will yell for you to stop. That's because OCD can't distinguish between danger and discomfort. Most of your triggers are unpleasant. Not dangerous. But, it's all the same to OCD.

If you let fear stop you, what will your life be like? Fear doesn't mean stop. If other people can go, so can you. Take the risk and go for it.

FEEL THE FEAR AND GO FOR IT

FEAR DOESN'T ALWAYS MEAN STOP. MOST THINGS ARE UNPLEASANT, NOT DANGEROUS. GO FOR IT!

I'VE GOT BETTER THINGS TO DO

It's not your choice or fault that you have OCD. But, it is your choice to feed it or starve it. If you feed it, then you're being bossed around by OCD. You're practicing avoidance and doing compulsions and mental acts such as rewinding, replaying and analyzing.

Compulsions or rituals can be stressful and lengthy. Many of them have to be restarted. Compulsions eat up time. You're late or too early getting to places. You're getting too little or too much sleep. Compulsions affect other people's time too. They're waiting for you to finish or they're taking the time to give you reassurance.

Sure, you might get temporary relief from performing a compulsion. But for how long? How many minutes or seconds before you have to do another compulsion? Meanwhile life is passing you by and your world is getting smaller.

Resist compulsive behaviors and do what you want or need to do. That's how you starve OCD. Starving it makes it weaker. Feeding it makes it stronger. If you feed it, you are choosing to make it stronger.

Do what you want to do. Live free.

I'VE GOT BETTER THINGS TO DO

DO WHAT YOU WANT TO DO NOT WHAT OCD WANTS YOU TO DO. LIVE FREE!

I CHOOSE WHAT TO FOCUS ON

One of the reasons mindfulness training is recommended in the treatment of OCD is because it develops the skill to focus on what matters. OCD is quite a chatterbox and without this skill, your attention will automatically go to OCD.

There are a number of ways to master the skill of focusing. Practice 10-20 minutes per day any one of these or a combination:

- Download meditation apps such as Calm, Headspace or Holosync

- Learn to juggle

- Coloring this book or any other coloring book can be helpful

- Select an object and notice everything about it. When your mind wanders say, "Ooops my mind just wandered." Then refer back to the [object.]

- Eat with all five senses. Think about how the food was grown and harvested

- Learn to play an instrument

You have the power to choose what to focus on. Do you want to focus on all the OCD thoughts? You don't have to. But, first you must develop the ability to shift your focus to what really matters in life.

I CHOOSE WHAT TO FOCUS ON

OCD CAN BE QUITE THE CHATTERBOX. BUT, YOU HAVE THE POWER TO CHOOSE WHAT TO FOCUS ON. CHOOSE!

COME ALONG WITH ME, OCD

OCD is portable. It goes wherever you go. It's a chaperone on steroids, always looking for danger. All it takes is for OCD to ask, "What if" or "What does this say about you?" or "What if you can't get this off your mind?" And boom, down the rabbit hole you go.

Thinking about triggers can occur without even being near one. Maybe you're not doing a compulsion at the moment, but thinking about doing the compulsion is happening right now.

What's the best way to handle the chatterbox?

- Hope and pray that OCD doesn't show up

- Check your thoughts to see if there's any OCD currently happening

- Scan the environment looking for triggers so that you can avoid them

- Just get some compulsions over with so you don't have it on your mind

You're right, none of the above.

It's so much more powerful to invite OCD to go wherever you go. It's going with you anyway. Why not show it you're in charge. Just invite it. That signals to OCD you don't care. And when OCD senses you don't care, it goes off duty.

WHATEVER HAPPENS, HAPPENS

¯_(☺)_/¯ This is the amazing remedy for OCD. It's not a cure but it is the way to counteract OCD. If you can shrug at OCD and say, "whatever" you're on your way to freeing your mind.

At first this is very difficult. Your feelings might not match the shrug. You're shrugging as if you don't care but you feel on fire—ready to explode. Keep shrugging. Fake it 'til you become it. OCD doesn't care about your feelings as much as it cares about your words and actions.

Remember the Cherokee tale of two wolves? There's a good wolf and a bad wolf. Which one wins? The one you feed. If OCD says go back, you go forward. If OCD says stop, you keep going. But, wow, if you add a shrug and a "whatever" that will really gives it some oomph.

If you don't shrug, and instead check to make sure everything is all right, you've just blown your chance at confidence. Checking only makes you become more unsure of yourself. You might get temporary relief but in the long run, that doesn't free your mind.

The more you tolerate doubt and shrug at uncertainty, the more confident you become. Shrugging makes you become more trusting. Resist checking. Tolerate the anxiety. It's not dangerous. It's just unpleasant. You can handle it. Endure the doubt. ¯_(☺)_/¯

WHATEVER HAPPENS, HAPPENS

YOU WILL NEVER BECOME CONFIDENT BY CHECKING. DON'T CHECK. WALK AWAY.

YOU CRACK ME UP, OCD

The reason OCD gets away with so much is because people take it so seriously. Everybody gets weird thoughts. But not everybody chuckles and says, "Wow, that was weird." What does weird mean? Is weird good or bad? Neither!

Something even better than calling your OCD thoughts weird or different is to actually laugh at the weird thoughts. I call my weird thoughts, "Dorpey Joes." It's funny sounding right? It's signaling to my brain I don't take these thoughts seriously. Laughing at OCD deflates it. It lets out all the air.

Even if it's hard to laugh at the thoughts, fake it. If you smile or even better laugh, your brain will register that maybe everything is okay. Of course OCD will test you and say, "Why are you laughing at such a horrible thought? Does this mean you are a horrible person?"

OCD is nothing but a liar. Fight fire with fire and lie right back. Act like the weird thoughts are funny, no matter how you really feel. Lie until your pants are on fire. Let go and laugh for 60 seconds, and when OCD questions why you're laughing, laugh harder.

Since laughter is one of the most powerful weapons against OCD, Google "Laughter Yoga University."

YOU CRACK ME UP, OCD

HUMOR IS THE MOST POWERFUL WEAPON YOU HAVE AGAINST OCD. LAUGH!

I'VE HAD ENOUGH OF YOU, OCD

OCD is actually desperately wanting you to take charge. It doesn't like being on duty 24/7. It's exhausting and the work is pointless and unrewarding. It's poking at you night and day so that you finally say, "ENOUGH is ENOUGH!"

Have someone poke you in the arm repeatedly and see how long you'll put up with it. How long before you say, "I've had enough of this!" What do you look like when you say it? What is your tone of voice. Do you sound like you mean it or are you begging, "Please stop."

Find your Super Pose. Chin up. Hands on your hips. Whatever your most powerful stance is, go into it and say, "I've had it with you OCD. Enough is enough. I"m taking charge." Don't imagine doing this. Do it! Literally Super Pose and show your grit.

What does it mean to be gritty?

G=Guts	The guts to feel the fear.
R=Rise Up	It's not the fall that matters. It's the getting up that counts!
I=Initiative	Initiate opportunities to be the boss and take charge.
T=Tenacity	If at first you don't succeed try, try again—be tenacious.

Or how about, Good Riddance I'm Taking Off. I've had enough, OCD!

PRACTICE MAKES PROGRESS

You get good at whatever you practice. If you practice doing compulsions, you'll get good at it. If you practice resisting compulsions, guess what? Right! You'll get good at resisting!

Make sure you identify your compulsions. Mental acts are the hardest to identify. Trying to get certainty by rewinding and replaying, analyzing your thoughts and feelings, mentally going through a ritual—those can all be compulsions. Once you've identified them, RESIST!

Even engaging in a dialogue with OCD can be a compulsion. The only thing you need to say to OCD is "Whatever. Who cares. So what." Just agree with it and you're on your way to freedom. But, don't engage in a back and forth discussion with OCD. RESIST!

Reassurance-seeking is another compulsion that feeds OCD. Reassurance-seeking is like alcohol to an alcoholic. It gives temporary relief but more and more of it is needed. If you're asking for reassurance, or reassuring yourself, you are feeding OCD. RESIST!

The more you resist the easier it gets. Practice saying NO to OCD. You'll be set free.

PRACTICE MAKES PROGRESS

PRACTICE RESISTING COMPULSIONS AND YOU'LL GET GOOD AT IT. FEEL A COMPULSION? JUST DON'T DO IT!

LIVING WITH UNCERTAINTY

The belief that there is such a thing as certainty is a lie. And, OCD the liar is very good at convincing you that you are more special than anybody else. That you, out of all the people in the world, can achieve certainty. It's a feat no one else has ever achieved. But, OCD says, "You can do it!"

It's actually very natural to have doubt. When you think about it, how can there be anything but? Yet, OCD the trickster, has you believing you are the one person in the entire world who shouldn't have to live with doubt. You are unique, but not nearly as special as OCD tells you.

No one on this earth has certainty. Everybody must live without it. You can't do enough to get certainty. No matter what compulsion you perform, you will still have doubt.

Maybe a compulsion tricks you into feeling certainty for the moment, but it won't last because it's not natural to live with certainty. It's impossible to achieve. And if OCD has its way, it will get you to spend a lifetime trying to achieve the impossible.

If you accept living with uncertainty, like the rest of the world, you'll be set free. You won't have to waste another moment trying to get something you can never have. Accept uncertainty and be free.

LIVING WITH UNCERTAINTY

WE CAN NEVER DO ENOUGH TO HAVE CERTAINTY. ACCEPT IT!

I'M PERFECTLY IMPERFECT

OCD makes you think you're special. It convinces you that you can be something no one else can be. There is no perfect person walking this earth today. No such person exists. And yet, OCD tells you that YOU can be perfect—that you should be perfect.

In an attempt to be perfect you spend far more hours on a task than necessary. You double, triple check your work. You look at yourself and find an inadequacy and think it must be rectified. Even though everybody is imperfect and inadequate—you have higher, unobtainable standards for yourself.

You hate to make mistakes and worry what people think of you. You want people's approval and try hard to get it. You strive for perfection—not excellence. It's not possible to achieve perfection, but OCD has you determined to get it.

When you agree, "I'm perfectly imperfect." When you agree to the truth, the pressure is off. You give OCD the message, "I don't care." There will be an internal conflict about whether or not you care, but fake it 'til you become it. Make mistakes on purpose.

Be willing to make mistakes. Accept the risk. Say, "WHATEVER!"

ACT AS IF YOU'RE NOT AFRAID

Your feelings are the problem not the solution. Don't wait to feel motivated or ready to take on OCD. If you wait for feelings to drive your behavior, you might not get very far.

Determination is a mindset, not an emotion.

You are anxious. That doesn't mean you can't move forward. If you wait until you're no longer afraid, you could be waiting a long, long time. Anxiety is in your blood. You've got to move forward despite the anxiety.

The more you move forward the more confident you become and yes, the less anxious you will be.

It's your reaction to anxiety that's causing the problem. Welcome the anxiety the same way you do on a rollercoaster ride or when watching a horror film or your favorite team playing in a championship game. Anxiety is a natural part of life.

OCD is lying to you. It tells you that you shouldn't do anything if you're afraid. Your goal must be to do what you want or need to do, even though you're anxious. Act like you're fine and accept the anxiety as an unpleasant nuisance.

Fake it 'til you become it.

I ACCEPT OCD

There is no cure for OCD. It's inconclusive what causes it. There is no magic pill. We have years of research ahead of us. In the meantime, how will you respond to OCD? The choice is to resist obsessions or accept them.

The treatment of OCD is to resist compulsions and ACCEPT obsessions. No matter how scary, real or uncomfortable the thought is—do nothing to get rid of the thought. If you resist the thought it will persist.

What can you resist? What must you resist? Compulsions. Rituals. Mental acts. Conversing with OCD. Reassurance-seeking. Avoiding triggers. None of this will free your mind. But, if you let the obsessions be, you're on a path to freedom.

Agree with the thoughts or at least be willing to say, "maybe." Respond to the obsessions with a shrug, "WHATEVER." If you're saying, "That's easier said than done" then you're not being honest about the current state of your life. How you're living right now isn't easy!

Let the obsessions be. Do nothing to resist them. This is how you free your mind…Free your life.

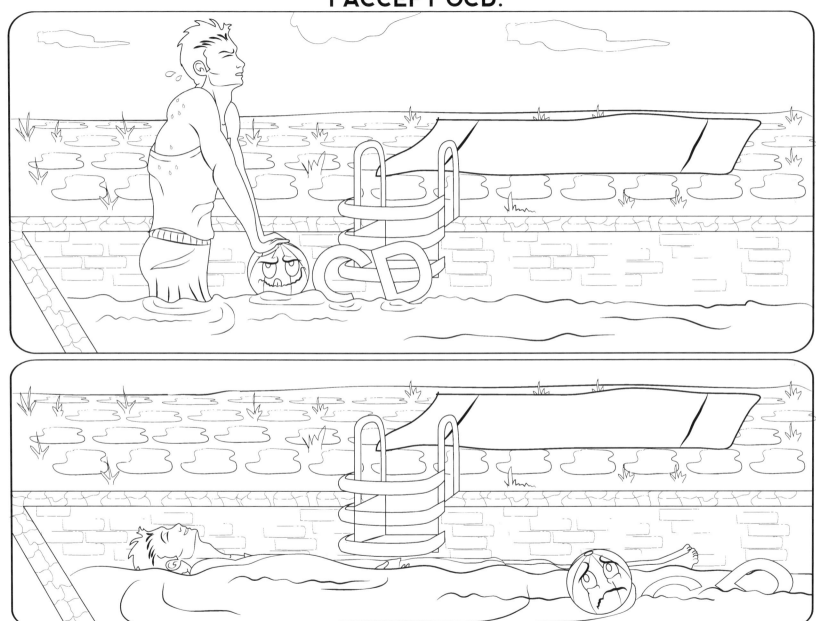

LET GO OR BE DRAGGED

There's something very controlling and rigid about OCD. It tells you a story about how you can control what happens in your life. OCD lies and says, "if you avoid this trigger or perform this compulsion, you'll have complete control over what happens."

If it were true that we could control what happens by performing a compulsion, then why isn't the military instructed on how to do compulsions? Why don't doctors throw out medicine and just give out compulsions to perform? Why don't we end poverty and world hunger with compulsions? Why don't parents teach their children to do compulsions to ward off anything bad happening?

OCD is trying to manage your anxiety by telling you a story. Within that story are a lot of things for you to try and control (i.e., compulsions.) OCD promises if you control these things your anxiety will go away. How's that working out?

Everybody has anxiety and discomfort. This effort to rid yourself of anxiety is a waste of time.

No one can control what happens. Not even you! The only thing you can control is how you react to what happens. If you keep trying to control what happens you'll be dragged.

Let go or be dragged.

ABOUT THE AUTHOR

Tammy LaBrake, is a Licensed Clinical Social Worker(LCSW) and founder of a private practice in New York called, Boss It Back® which is dedicated to the treatment of OCD.

As an unorthodox thinker, she values cutting edge developments. Knowing how important mindful exercises are in the treatment of OCD, Tammy created this coloring book to help people stay focused on the strategies that are most effective.

With years of experience, coupled with training by the best in the field, Tammy is known as a regional expert in the treatment of OCD. She is a member of the International OCD Foundation and is a graduate of the Foundation's Behavior Training Therapy Institute.

To learn more about defying OCD visit Tammy's website at ocdstrategies.com and read her weekly blog at blog.bossitback.com.

To enhance the coloring experience and to help implement each strategy, order these two supplemental add-ons: The "Companion Course to The OCD Coloring Book" and "The OCD Coloring Book Journal." Visit OCDstrategies.com for more information on how to order these fun and helpful add-ons.

GO FOR IT

USE YOUR POWER

LIVE FREE

CHOOSE

INVITE IT

WALK AWAY

LAUGH

TAKE CHARGE

JUST DON'T DO IT

WHATEVER

ACCEPT IT
LET GO OR BE DRAGGED
LET IT BE
FAKE IT 'TILL YOU BECOME IT

Made in the USA
Coppell, TX
23 January 2020